GETTING A GRIP

Build a *custom* parenting plan that actually *works*

Bethany Meadows

Cover design: Marianne Beard
Cover image: Getty Images, www.istockphoto.com
Interior layout by: Anthony Guin
Edited by: Ann Marie Harvey
Printed in the United States of America
Scripture quotations are from the NIV version of the Bible.

First Printing, 2017
ISBN-13:
978-0692987032 (Vertical Solutions Media Inc)
ISBN-10:
0692987037

For questions, or to request copies please contact:
Vertical Solutions Media
5637 Myron Clark Rd
McCalla AL 35111
Fax: 877-200-5204

Dedication

It is from my precious mom, Debbie Bowman,
I learned first-hand about grace, compassion and
endless patience. She has always been the Godly
example I could turn to when I lost my way. Without
her gentle spirit, this rebellious and crazy kid would
not have made it to adulthood. She is my rock.

It is because of the support of my husband,
Jeff Meadows, I found the courage to finish
writing this book. When the one you love believes
in you, it means everything. Thank you for all
you do for our family.

Every challenge, every experience, every blessed
moment as a mother has been my privilege.
Without my children, life would have been silent,
organized and cold. It is my greatest joy to see you
find your purpose in God's plan for you.

Table of Contents

Introduction

Parenting is one of life's greatest responsibilities and one of its most daunting challenges. If you have a child who is more than five minutes old, you already know what I'm talking about.

I probably read a hundred parenting books in my quest to figure out the answers I needed with all the situations I faced with my own five children and two stepchildren. I decided early on that it would be wise to seek out all the help I could get. I also found out that while they were helpful in some areas, many of those books just didn't understand the specific dynamic of my unique family.

I soon learned there is not a one-size-fits-all parenting model. Just when you think you've got them figured out, they seem to suddenly evolve and you end up wondering just who that alien creature is sitting at your kitchen table.

As they grow, they enter new phases of their development, leaving you to decide by what rules you now need to play. Then you find out that as they develop every child's needs are different. When you raise one teenager and you think you are prepared for the second...think again. Every stage seems to be an entirely different experience with each child.

In addition, parents are people too. That means we are unique individuals with personalities and value systems that also affect the dynamics of a family.

Being a parent is the toughest job you will face. It will bring you some of your deepest joys and your most intense pain. It often feels like a roller coaster ride complete with thrills, chills, twists, and turns...and a few screams for good measure.

I never set out to write a book that would tell you how to raise your children. That is ultimately between you and God. However, I do hope that this book will provide a guideline with which you can build your own framework for a parenting plan. One that you can customize for the individual and unique needs of your family.

Your children are your responsibility. Not your neighbors. Not your village. Not your government. Not even your church. Don't allow anyone or anything to be the primary influencer of their values and character. I believe God will ask me to answer for my parenting choices one day. I want to be able to say that I followed His instructions, sought His guidance when I got stuck and remained steadfast when the journey got tough. I call it "staying vertical" and it's a motto I keep close to my heart.

There is no one who knows your child better than you. Not a teacher. Not a coach. Not this book. Take all advice both in these pages and elsewhere through the filter of that basic principle. In other words, take what works for your family and leave the rest.

Peace I leave with you;

My peace I give to you;

not as the world gives do I give to you.

Do not let your heart be troubled,

nor let it be fearful.

John 14:27

Chapter 1

Get Your Head Right

Let's forget your sweet little angels for just a moment and start with you. Yes, I'm talking to you. Building your home begins with a solid foundation.

You are not perfect. In fact, if you're like most humans, you likely have some things about you that are downright cracked or broken. This is because your parents had things about them that were also cracked or broken that they passed along to you.

If you were raised in a dysfunctional environment it will impact the way you parent. The truth is that many people don't know how to parent effectively because they didn't have a good role model to follow themselves. If you want to raise your children successfully, then start with looking at your own issues so that you can be free to become a positive role model.

Many people don't make the connection between their issues and how it affects their ability to be a good parent.

YOU HAVE ISSUES. WE ALL HAVE ISSUES.

My pastor is fond of saying that everyone has issues. If you don't think you have issues, that IS your issue. The first step to overcoming a problem within yourself is accepting that you have a problem and really looking at it from an objective viewpoint.

Many people don't make the connection between their issues and how it affects their ability to be a good parent. However, they can be a huge stumbling block. If you have anger, pride or any other struggles in your character, you will be ineffective at best and abusive at worst in dealing with your children. For their sake and yours, deal with your issues.

- **Go to counseling.** If you have ever been physically, mentally or sexually abused, find a professional to help you work through it. Suppressing this kind of hurt is dangerous to your emotional and spiritual well-being. Holding on to the past will hurt you, your marriage and your children. There is no shame in getting help to make sense of your past. And, there is victory in coming to terms with it. Make an appointment right now and begin your journey to true healing.

- **Offer forgiveness.** It is said that forgiveness is not for the benefit of the person who harmed you, but rather a gift to yourself. If you do not truly forgive when needed, you will struggle with resentment and bitterness, both of which will come out in the way you parent your children. This can be especially true if you have gone through divorce and are bitter toward your ex-spouse.

- **Share your struggle.** You don't have to tell the world your private business, but be willing to share your struggles with someone you trust. Isolating yourself in your struggles is overwhelming and lonely. Don't let pride get in the way of leaning on someone and letting them help you move past whatever obstacles you are experiencing.

- **Don't overcompensate.** Sometimes parents are so impacted by something in their childhood that they overcompensate with their own children. For example, someone raised in poverty might spoil their child with material things or someone raised in a strict controlling environment might decide not to provide their children with any boundaries. If you've ever said "when I have kids, I will never…," you just might be overcompensating somewhere. Be aware of your over-compensating behavior and work toward a balance for it.

- **Be honest with yourself.** Denial is a powerful emotion and can blind you to the truth. Be willing to be honest with your limitations, your baggage and your blunders. No one is perfect but we can be aware of our faults and take steps to resolve issues instead of being doomed to repeat mistakes. Don't be afraid to apologize to your kids when you are wrong. Everyone makes mistakes and this only models for them the right thing to do when they do something wrong.

Parenting is hard work. There is no magic pill and no perfect answer. To be successful, you must do the right thing for your child even when it makes you feel bad, you are too tired to think and it seems like no one appreciates your efforts.

> *"Live so that when your children think of fairness*
> *and integrity, they think of you."*
> —*H. Jackson Brown*

SET THE RIGHT EXAMPLE.

Your children look to you for an example to follow. In fact, they will learn many of their basic skills just by watching you—walking, talking, eating, etc. They will also learn how to respond to conflict, frustration and anger in the very same way.

Actions speak louder than words. If you are a yeller, they will probably yell. If you hit, they will think hitting is acceptable. If you disrespect them or others, they will be disrespectful to those around them.

Children will also yell, hit and disrespect because they haven't yet attained a full grasp of their emotions. You don't have that excuse. You are the adult. You are the example. If you come unglued every time your child has a temper tantrum, they are never going to see an alternative way to act.

Keeping your cool while your kids are acting out, arguing with you, rolling their eyes and other disrespectful body language is not easy. It takes practice AND having a solid parenting plan in place. If your only plan is to fuss at them over and over, smack them in the heat of the moment or ignore their behavior as long as possible, then you are probably going to have trouble remaining calm or in control of anything. Have a plan and stick to the plan no matter what. (Wondering how to make a plan? We'll cover that later in the book.)

My issues were a heap of trouble for me because they fed off each other. I was a yeller (learned behavior from my dad), a control freak AND I was consumed with fear that I was doing everything wrong and messing up my kids. The fear drove my controlling nature and when things didn't work out the way I thought they should, I yelled.

My turning point moment of change came when I found myself shouting into the sweet, wide-eyed and terrified face of my then eight-year-old daughter. I had completely lost control of my emotions and was acting like a crazy person. The look on her face was like a knife to my heart. I mumbled an apology and left the room for the solace of my walk-in closet, more than a few tears and some earnest time of prayer acknowledging before God that I needed to change.

I'm thankful that today I know how to claim victory over my emotions. While my need to control my circumstances still makes my eye twitch now and then, I've learned to appreciate the peace that comes with going-with-the-flow and adjusting my rigid expectations. Through prayer and focusing on bettering myself for the sake of my family, I trust more and fear less. All of this has meant a more peaceful home and children who could trust that no matter what they did, mom could hold herself together.

INVEST IN YOUR MARRIAGE

Your marriage is the cornerstone of your family. Through your relationship with your spouse your children will see and learn conflict resolution, compromise, intimacy and so much more. Investing in your marriage should be a priority every day.

Your spouse is your parenting partner and it's important that you are both on the same page.

If you are having problems in your marriage, get help. I don't think I need to explain this one. It should be obvious.

Your spouse is your parenting partner and it's important that you are both on the same page. Children know how to play both sides to their advantage so having a united front is an important defense. Talk through your parental plan until you both agree on it. Keep each other accountable to following the plan consistently and allow each other to play the roles you have agreed upon without interference from the other.

If you are like most couples, you and your spouse have different personalities that complement each other. Instead of letting that become a point of conflict in your parenting plan, provide each parent with the roles that best suit their skills and temperament.

Parenting is hard. It's important to support your spouse in their efforts even when not perfectly executed. Understand that you are both a work in progress and neither of you is perfect. If you disagree or argue in front of your kids, be respectful to one another. Let it be an opportunity to model how to disagree without being disrespectful. If one of you makes a decision, the other should back them up. Undermining your spouse with your children is about as productive as taking a sledgehammer to the foundation of your house. Eventually it will cause serious structural damage.

If you are divorced, then having a like-minded parenting plan with your ex-spouse is going to require lots of patience, compromise and willpower to stay on track.

> *There are very few certainties that touch us all in this mortal experience, but one of the absolutes is that we will experience hardship and stress at some point.*
> *– Dr. James C. Dobson*

MANAGE YOUR STRESS.

Stress falls into two categories—positive and negative. There are some things that stress us but have a positive result—things like deadlines that help keep us accountable or a difficult problem at work that allows us to feel fulfilled when we solve it. However, when stress increases above a level that we are used to, it can have some pretty serious adverse effects.

When you are stressed your body has a similar reaction as to when it senses you are in danger. It speeds up your heart and your breathing by releasing chemicals into your system. All of this will lead to an instinctive response to either stand and fight or run and hide depending on the individual.

If stress is allowed to continue for too long or too often

in your life, your health can suffer. Headaches, insomnia, stomach problems and muscle pain are all common physical responses to stress. In addition, it can weaken your immune system making you vulnerable to other health problems as well.

If you are not healthy or operating your life in a healthy way, your ability to be a parent will be diminished. A stressed parent will be more short-tempered and make poor parenting decisions in the heat of the moment.

If you are not healthy or operating your life in a healthy way, your ability to be a parent will be diminished.

TAKE CONTROL OF YOUR LIFE.

Stress Strategy #1 – Just say NO. Learn that it is perfectly acceptable NOT to volunteer to bring the snacks, to organize the carpool or to teach that Sunday School class. We live in an age and culture of busy. Let's all take a stand against excessive busyness and start saying "no" to the things that are making us run around frantically. Wouldn't it be worth it if we could master the ability to manage our lives more effectively?

Stress Strategy #2 – Manage time. There are only 24 hours in a day. Try removing things from your life that waste one of your most precious commodities. One area I cut when my kids were young was television. Television consumes our precious time without an adequate return for the investment. Instead we had Netflix and were purposeful about what we watched and when. Think about what is sucking up your time. Get rid of it or reduce its impact on your time.

Stress Strategy #3 – Identify priorities. Trying to cram in as much stuff as possible leaves no time to clear your head or relax. When my kids were younger I tried to involve us only in things we could do as a family. Instead of each child having their own pursuits, we hosted study groups, took Tae Kwon Do classes as a family and went to the park or spent the weekend camping. While dance and soccer are nice for a season, I feel like we reduced everyone's stress while improving our connection as a family by focusing on our time together. If one of the kids did do something on their own like soccer, they each took turns to help reduce the mania and the entire family supported them by attending every game and cheering them on. If you feel like you are too busy, try first scheduling time with your spouse, then time together as a family and then see what time you have left for individual extracurricular activities. If your priority is your family, your calendar should reflect it.

WHAT ABOUT STRESS CAUSED BY THINGS WE DON'T CONTROL?

Whether you face divorce, death or a significant loss, if you are walking this earth for any period of time you are going to have to deal with a heart-breaking situation at some point and time.

When I first learned that my husband of 17 years was having an affair, the shock of it hit me like a freight train. Unless you've walked that particular path, I could never adequately explain the pain, the anxiety and the stress that it causes. When he left to pursue and ultimately marry the object of his affection, the resulting stress caused rapid and significant weight loss, about a third of my hair fell out and my brain lost memory and the ability to focus on anything longer than five minutes. While you may never experience this exact situation (and I hope you don't), life WILL throw us a curve ball every now and then. The following is what I learned in my personal journey that helped me get through a very difficult and stressful situation. I pray that you might find them useful if you ever find yourself facing down your own curve ball.

- **Forgive.** Often stress caused by things outside of our control is the result of the actions of someone else. Staying angry and becoming bitter will only hurt your ability to move past it. Or perhaps you need to forgive yourself for a mistake or bad decision. You're human—cut yourself some slack. If you struggle to forgive, seek some counseling to help you work through the situation.

- **Ask a trusted friend for help.** This one has always been hard for me. Pride generally gets in the way of reaching out. If not for the good friend that walked me through this dark time, I know that I would not have made it to the other side with my heart and soul intact.

- **Get professional attention, if needed.** If you are unable to sleep, are experiencing fluttering in your chest, have the sensation that your heart is in your throat, are finding it hard to take a deep breath (shallow breathing) or are having trouble keeping food down, it is time to get to a doctor. There is help and if left untreated these symptoms can become a real and serious threat to your health.

- **Write it down.** Within 24 hours of learning about the affair, I began writing a journal. I wrote down everything that came to mind, whether it made sense in the moment or not. Sometimes I stayed up all night writing in that journal. It became a close confidant and was a very healthy way for me to express the tidal wave of emotion that was threatening to wash me away.

- **Focus on the future.** Circumstances are temporary. True joy comes from knowing that God is bigger than our problems and that He cares for us. Some nights I fell asleep singing "Jesus Loves Me" over and over. The lyrics to this simple children's song were so affirming that they soothed and healed my wounded spirit with every word.

- **Be courageous.** Do not allow fear to take over. In difficult circumstances you will no doubt be facing some hard decisions. Gather your courage and do what you need to do. Guard yourself from having wrong motives or making a bad decision out of fear, anger or revenge. At the end of the day, do what is right and good for you, your family and anyone else affected. Do not adopt a victim mentality. Claim victory over your problems and move forward.

As a parent, you have the responsibility of running your household, providing for your family and raising your children. Your ability to do that well is directly impacted by your mental and emotional well-being. If you neglect to take care of yourself, you won't be able to care for anyone else.

But as for me and my household,

we will serve the LORD.

Joshua 24:15

Chapter 2

Decide Who You Will Serve

The idea that we are created by God for a plan and a purpose is more than just a feel-good Sunday morning sermon title! Allowing God to take first place in our life means He should also have first place in our family. Raising kids who are confident in their identity in Christ requires us to make a decision. Who will we serve?

Our kids are under attack and many parents are completely unaware. Entertainment, social media, academia and culture are now major contributors to helping our kids decide right from wrong. And mostly the message is "if it feels good to you, then it's not wrong." Breaking down the absolute morals of right and wrong is how Satan can get a foothold in your child's life.

Most parents can agree that their child's belief system

> ## *The gap between our faith and the world we now live in is wide, twisting and complicated.*

will be challenged at some point. Are you confident in knowing what those challenges look like and how to talk about them with your kids?

The gap between our faith and the world we now live in is wide, twisting and complicated. This can leave us parenting from a place of fear and frustration.

While the world around us is ever-changing, God's Word and His ways remain constant. Thank goodness we can depend on Him to be our steady Rock and provide guidance for us as we lead our children down the path that God has purposed for them.

RAISING GODLY KIDS IN AN UNGODLY WORLD

1. Focus on our own faith.

If we are not equipped spiritually, how can we be in a position to equip our kids? More than just understanding the basics, we have to learn how to defend the Christian faith and answer the tough cultural questions of today.

It's not enough to know WHAT you believe but also WHY you believe it. Why does a loving God allow suffering or send someone to hell? What evidence is there for a God? Is the Bible relevant for today when it was written so long ago? If you are not answering these questions for your kids, somebody somewhere will do it for you and it's possible it will not be in a Biblical way.

Being versed in Christian apologetics will help you defend your faith and teach your kids about how to defend theirs.

2. Live it out as an example.

Your children are much more likely to do as you DO rather than what you say. If you tell them one version of right and wrong but are modeling another, you will lose all credibility. We cannot make exceptions for ourselves based on circumstances or feelings in the moment and then expect our kids to stand alone when their friends invite them to make a bad choice.

Our kids desperately need to see us study God's Word, be the hands and feet of Jesus and live out our faith in the way we spend our money and time. Even more than that, they need us to bring them along for the journey.

3. Be their primary spiritual leader.

Raising kids to discover and follow God's purpose for their life is OUR responsibility. While they can be a wonderful influence, their youth leaders, teachers, coaches, neighbors and other family members are not tasked specifically by God to teach your children. God will ask you to answer for how intentional you were with the precious gifts He put in your care.

Anything that is important and worthwhile deserves some forethought and a plan. The goal of Godly kids should be a high priority and reflected in the effort we put into it.

Recently a friend's son was diagnosed with juvenile diabetes. His very life suddenly became dependent on her and her husband's ability to understand the role nutrition and a necessary medication regimen now played on his health. Imagine if my friend decided that she was too busy to take the time to care properly for her son's physical need. The consequences would be devastating to his health and possibly even his life.

In the same way, our kids' spiritual health is dependent upon our commitment to being a spiritual leader. That means being their source for spiritual truths and paying attention so we know when they need us to come alongside them.

4. **Study the Bible together.**

Statistics show fewer than one in 10 Christian families study the Bible together in a given week. Most Christian parents agree that studying the Bible is important but life has a way of distracting us from this priority. If your kids perceive that the Bible is on the back burner, they'll have little reason to see it as important.

The more we talk with our kids, the more they are equipped for what they hear in the world. Make time for those teachable moments when they come up. The time of their youth will pass quickly, so take advantage of every opportunity to invest in their knowledge of God's Word.

5. **Teach your kids how to love.**

We are raising kids in an angry and entitled world. Every child regardless of age can practice the Biblical principles of forgiveness, love and generosity. Talk with them about ways they can love others right where they are. The simple lesson of showing love to others is one they will carry with them into adulthood.

One of the reasons God brings two people together in marriage is to raise Godly children. It is a responsibility that should be given high priority as we consider that God has a plan and a purpose for each of our children. It is our job to train and teach them God's ways in preparation for the great things He has planned.

While your first instinct might be to put your kids in a bubble, our goal shouldn't be to simply minimize their exposure to the things of the world. Instead do life alongside them, alert them to the challenges and equip them with what they need to be confident in their faith.

Train up a child in the

way he should go;

even when he is old he

will not depart from it.

Proverbs 22:6

Chapter 3

Build an Intentional Parenting Plan

When you open a business, you write out business and marketing plans to establish your goals and objectives and figure out the best road to future success. These plans explore everything from budget, expected return on investments, competitor analysis and so on.

Being a parent has many parallels to owning a business. When your child is born they are just a great new idea, full of potential just waiting to be nurtured and grown.

While not all businesses go the distance, those that are successful almost always have a business and marketing plan that they have drafted, followed and revised from time to time. As the saying goes, "If you fail to plan, then you plan to fail." Why would something like parenting be any different?

God created man with a higher purpose and with that comes a responsibility to raise our children to know and appreciate His plan and calling on their lives.

DEVELOP A PARENTING PLAN.

Somewhere along the way, many of us bought into the idea that parenting would just come naturally. You know, there's the suggestion that we are all born with the instincts needed to successfully raise our brood. I've got news for you! That idea may be true for monkeys and gophers where instincts are essential to survival of the species, but here in our human reality, nothing could be further from the truth.

The problem with that idea is that we possess more than just instincts. Our existence goes beyond survival. God created man with a higher purpose and with that comes a responsibility to raise our children to know and appreciate His plan and calling on their lives.

Many parents have never taken the time to consider their parenting objectives—the things we strive to teach our children before they are grown. If you do not know where you are going, any road will take you there. However, if you develop goals and objectives, you become intentional about devising a plan or strategy that will bring those things you want for your children to fruition.

Of course, we all want our children to be well-behaved, happy and successful at life. However, within every family those terms are bound to be defined in very different ways. I believe parenting objectives need to be specific and the strategy for attaining them unique for every family.

What are your parenting objectives?

Take a moment to consider what is really important to you for your children right now. Is it that they are the most popular at school, the best player on the team or that they hit the honor roll every semester? Let's try again. What is really important to you for your children that will continue to impact their lives 10, 20 and 50 years from now? Did that change your answer?

With the long-term in mind, try and develop at least five specific parenting objectives for your children. The following are some of my parenting objectives to help get you started in your thought process:

a) To understand the importance of serving others.

b) To be grateful for their blessings and content with what they possess.

c) To understand that forgiveness and mercy are gifts to

be given generously.

d) To take personal responsibility for their actions and accept consequences with grace.

f) To have a strong work ethic and do everything with excellence.

Having parenting objectives changes everything.

When we understand our true long-term objectives as a parent, it changes the way we choose to spend our time and resources. Our priorities shift as we focus on things that truly matter in the long run and put less emphasis on the here and now. Are you ready to start raising a generation that will change the world or are you content with giving them the status quo?

What are your family's top five values? List them here in order of importance.

1.

2.

3.

4.

5.

Now take your number one answer above and come up with three ways your children would help fulfill those values. For example, if you value close family relationships, you might list that you want your kids to be respectful, kind or have a servant's heart.

1.

2.

3.

Once you understand what you truly want for your children, you can better understand how to build a parenting plan that will head them in the right direction.

- If you want children who are grateful and appreciative, stop buying them every toy, gadget and gizmo.

- If you want children who are respectful, don't allow them to talk back, argue or make inappropriate gestures like rolling their eyes, sighing loudly or throwing out a hip without a consequence.

- If you want children who are self-assured, be consistent so they always know what to expect.

- If you want children who are unselfish, don't make them the center of the universe.

- If you want children who love others, give them regular

opportunities to serve their family and their community.

When I first brought home an adopted sibling group of four children, we went from one to five children overnight. They had been in and out of the foster care system for a number of years. They had never learned respect. They focused on getting what they wanted, when they wanted it and would run over anyone who got in their way. They threw the mother-of-all temper tantrums. Ever seen an 11-year-old throw down on the ground and pitch a fit? It's not pretty.

While most families are not built in such an instantaneous fashion, some of you may be at this point right now with your children. You might even be thinking it's too late to change because they are older. I'm here to say it's never too late.

My first objective was respect. Without it, we could not function as a family. It was foundational to our success as a family and I drove toward it with everything in my parenting arsenal. I made a plan to address the lack of respect they were showing and I stuck to my plan. It did not happen in a day or even a week, but soon they learned that I was going to require respect from them with no exceptions. Once we had a handle on respect, we moved on to other objectives and tackled them one at a time.

A wise child accepts

a parent's discipline;

a mocker refuses

to listen to correction.

Proverbs 13:1

Chapter 4

Establish House Rules

Rules are a necessary part of life. Without the rules of the road, more people would die in accidents. Without rules at school, people would not learn. Without rules in your home, you will not find peace.

Just like with the rules of the road, the more people who are involved, the more rules are needed. If we only had one driver on the road, we wouldn't need rules. The more cars on the road, the more rules are needed to keep everyone safe.

The same is true of your home. If you have only one child, you will have fewer rules than if you have a large family. Rules are put into place to keep us safe and teach us right from wrong. They are important.

This is your house. You make the rules and guidelines. You and your spouse need to agree on what rules you want

Without rules in your home, you will not find peace.

for your family and your kids shouldn't get a vote (their brains are too small). They should be general enough to cover varying situations yet specific enough so they are not too vague or confusing (again, small brains need things simple).

We used *The 21 Rules of This House* by Gregg Harris (www.greggharrisblog.blogspot.com). You can search online at amazon.com or other retailers for the coloring book and jelly-proof sign for your fridge. We did and it was awesome.

The 21 Rules of This House are as follows:

1. We obey God.

2. We love, honor and pray for one another.

3. We tell the truth.

4. We consider one another's interests ahead of our own.

5. We speak quietly and respectfully with one another.

6. We do not hurt one another with unkind words or deeds.

7. When someone needs correction, we correct him in love.

8. When someone is sorry, we forgive him.

9. When someone is sad, we comfort him.

10. When someone is happy, we rejoice with him.

11. When we have something nice to share, we share it.

12. When we have work to do, we do it without complaining.

13. We take good care of everything that God has given us.

14. We do not create unnecessary work for others.

15. When we open something, we close it.

16. When we take something out, we put it away.

17. When we turn something on, we turn it off.

18. When we make a mess, we clean it up.

19. When we do not know what to do, we ask.

20. When we go out, we act just as if we were in this house.

21. When we disobey or forget any of the 21 Rules of This House, we accept the discipline and instruction of the Lord.

You don't have to use the above list. The rules you use are up to you. Just make sure you actually have some established rules. Post them on the fridge. Talk about them with your kids to reinforce what they are and why they are important to follow. Let them know which rule they are have broken when you give them a consequence.

One of my kids once came in from roller blading

outside to use the rest room. She decided that she'd just roll right through the house instead of taking them off. When I stopped her she smugly told me that there was no rule that covered roller blading in the house. I pointed to Rule #13 and then shared how blessed I felt that the Lord had provided us with beautiful hardwood floors and that I expected her to take care of them. (Nice try, kiddo.) Without posted rules, I'd just be arguing with a child who would spend her energy trying to convince me why roller blades in the house should be permissible.

Take your spouse out for coffee where you will have no distractions and brainstorm what family rules you would like to implement. Be sure you also know how you will handle consequences for broken rules ahead of time. The heat of the moment is not the best time to decide the fate of your roller blading offender.

Now that you have your rules, post them in a central location. Advise the kids to take a good look because they are responsible for knowing and abiding by the rules.

GUIDELINES

It's also necessary to have some "guidelines" to help keep things running smoothly. I often added guidelines following a specific situation or problem. By way of example, some of my guidelines were as follows:

- Assigned seats: Having assigned seats in the car, at the

table, in church, etc., completely avoided the "shotgun" arguments in the car or fighting over who sat where at every meal. It also allowed me to place my "chatty" or "mischievous" children right next to me in church.

- Schedule expectations: As a homeschool family we needed structure to our schedule or we would never have finished all the school work for each day. The kids were expected to get up on their own (setting their own alarm clock), get dressed, eat breakfast and be sitting at their desk by 8:00 a.m. They received a ticket for every five minutes they were late. This is reasonable starting around age nine or 10, while children who are younger might need some help getting up, etc.

- No morning showers: Only adults were allowed to take morning showers. Hey, with this many kids in the house it was the only way I would ever get a hot shower! Besides, cold showers make me grumpy, especially before coffee.

Guidelines are those things that just make sense for operating your household. While it was a big problem in our house, maybe your kids never fight about who gets to sit where so assigned seats wouldn't make sense for you. Guidelines are a great way to create a consistent process in a problem area in order to achieve more peace and unity.

No such thing as a credible threat

Recently I overheard a mom speaking to her daughter in the shoe department. Mom was trying on shoes while her very bored four-year-old was knocking shoes off the shelf. Mom asked her not to knock shoes off the shelf. (This did not work.) She then asked the daughter repeatedly if she wanted a spanking. "Do you want a spanking?" "Is that what you want?" "Why do you want a spanking?" (For the record, I'm pretty sure daughter was not concerned about a spanking taking place and she was right.) Then mom had a "why are you acting this way" one-way discussion with herself because daughter was too busy ramping up her whining and shoe tossing to hear any more hollow threats. Finally in a moment of desperation, mom promises daughter ice cream if she stops whining. Daughter immediately stopped whining and they left to get ice cream. Kid = 1 | Mom = 0

I'm not judging. We've all been there. That moment where your will has been worn down by the incessant whining and mindless arguing of a four-year-old that you'd do just about anything to make it stop. Forgive yourself, move on and next time see if grandma can babysit when you need to buy yourself some shoes. At the very least, stop threatening consequences if you have no intention of following through.

Bottom line…
DON'T MAKE THREATS: "If you do that again, I'll…"
You'll what? Your kids know you're not serious. You are only

Words have power.
They can injure or they can inspire.

damaging your credibility with those empty threats. And, it's likely they are even laughing at you behind that angelic face. If you are not going to follow through on a statement, don't say it in the first place. Consequences for behavior should already be laid out for your kids so there is no need to keep saying it in the form of hollow threats over and over

DO SAY WHAT YOU MEAN: If you want your children to believe what you say, then say what you mean and mean what you say. If you want to give them a warning, ask them once to correct their behavior, then immediately follow through with the consequences if they don't. Put some substance into your words and your kids are less likely to ignore them.

The power of words.

> *Sticks and stones may break my bones,*
> *but words can never hurt me.*

Words have power. They can injure or they can inspire. We can get so focused on the words coming from our children, yet so easily forget to watch the words coming from our own mouths.

DON'T PUT THEM DOWN: Words hurt. Listen to how you speak to your kids. Have you ever used phrases like "Are you stupid or something?" "You are such a disappointment!" "Don't be an idiot!" or something similar? These kinds of statements are sending the wrong messages and are born out of frustration and not discipline. The fact is that kids are going to make bad decisions and make mistakes. It's time to stop being surprised when it happens and just learn how to deal with it when they do.

DO DEVELOP POSITIVE PHRASES: In the heat of the moment, words are spoken which are first to mind. For that reason you need to develop some positive alternatives that you can draw from when you are feeling angry or frustrated with your child. My warning line was "Would you like to rephrase?" You and your spouse should pick whatever line works for the two of you. Having a warning line allows you to teach your child to think through what happened and find a better choice for the next time. If you need to calm down first then just say "I'm upset right now. We will talk about this when I calm down." It's ok to be human.

Keeping your cool.

Anger is a normal human emotion. God created our emotions so it's ok to be angry. However, God also warned us not to sin in our anger. In Ephesians 4:26, the apostle Paul says, "In your anger do not sin." The New Living Translation has a great way of stating it: "And don't sin by letting anger control you."

Kids have a way of working that one last nerve. They seem to know when we're having a bad day and zero in and try our patience in the most annoying ways possible. My kids have made me so angry that my blood pressure would spike, causing me to see red spots. I now know from personal experience where the saying "seeing red" comes from.

Regardless, you are the adult, which means you have to try to do better.

DON'T YELL OR LOSE YOUR TEMPER: When you yell, scream or lose control, your kids no longer hear your words. All they hear is anger and now they are processing that instead of what you are shouting at them. It raises their anxiety and whatever lesson, however brilliant, that you might be spewing has been completely lost in the noise. It's ineffective and it will leave YOU feeling stressed out. If you do lose control, you should apologize. This is your chance to model the right response to making a mistake.

DO MODEL SELF CONTROL: The bottom line is your anger is irrelevant. Kids can SEE you are angry, frustrated or annoyed without having to witness you coming unglued. It is not a bad thing for them to see that you have emotions. However, this is your opportunity to model the kind of behavior that you want your children to use when they have those feelings. Do you want them to lose their temper with their little sister when she does something to make them angry? Probably not. Most parents would agree they want to see their children learn conflict resolution skills. That begins with you SHOWING them it in action.

Remove the helicopter landing pad.

Rescuing your children from their own irresponsible choices will quickly become a full-time job if you don't allow them the natural consequences of their mistakes. I had one child who was particularly forgetful, which constantly created "emergencies." After I began allowing the consequences of their forgetfulness, their memory greatly improved. Funny how that works.

The problem for most of us is that we worry about those consequences, sometimes more than our kids do. What if they lose a job? Get in trouble at school? Lose a friend? I would argue the more important question is how will they become responsible adults, if they are not required to be responsible now?

DON'T BE A RESCUER: You know who you are. We have all been that parent at some point. The one who swoops down and saves little Johnny every time he makes a mistake. He forgets his lunch and you bring it to him. He gets in trouble at school and you insist to the administrator there must be some kind of mistake. He gets benched at soccer and you have words with the coach. I have a friend who fired a 26-year-old man for missing days of work without calling in and being chronically late. <u>His mother</u> called later that day to demand an explanation. Did I mention the employee was 26? There is no nice way to tell you this. If you are a rescuer, STOP! Little Johnny is one day going to spread his wings and fly into this cold, cruel world and if you keep rescuing him, he will struggle to succeed.

<u>**DO**</u> PROTECT AND SUPPORT: Natural consequences provide some of life's best lessons. If you interfere, you have robbed your child of the experience. It is much better that you allow minor consequences to happen so that your child will become a responsible and careful adult. If he forgets his lunch, let him go hungry for one day. Chances are the hunger pains will be the only lesson he needs and he will not likely forget his lunch again. Introduce a new phrase into your vocabulary: "Gee, that's a bummer, Johnny. What are you going to do?" Let them figure it out. For younger children, give two or three suggestions of how you would handle it and then let them decide. If they are older, just let them decide. However, there ARE times when you must interfere to protect your children from consequences that are dangerous. Knowing when to act is the balancing act that we must all learn as parents.

Failure to plan is a plan to fail.

Most of us plan for retirement, plan our vacations or plan our kid's birthday parties. Yet so many parents don't have a plan for discipline. It's important that kids know the rules and the consequences ahead of time. It's not fair to expect them to read your mind or worse, figure out the rules when they depend on your mood.

DON'T SHOOT FROM THE HIP: So many parents just deal with kid issues as they come. They have no real plan or strategy and consequences are usually dealt on a whim and during emotional duress.

DO DEVELOP A PLAN: Yes, it will take work. Parenting is hard work. Making a plan is an investment in your children and in your own sanity. If you have a plan you will easily know how to handle almost every situation.

Shooting from the hip in the heat of the moment is just too subjective to your mood, emotions, or, let's face it, how much sleep you got the night before. By having a plan, no matter how you feel in the moment you have a clear cut way to address behavior in a calm and reasonable fashion.

Establish House Rules

All Scripture is breathed out

by God and profitable for teaching,

for reproof, for correction,

and for training in righteousness,

that the man of God may be competent,

equipped for every good work.

2 Timothy 3:16-17

Chapter 5

Develop a Discipline Strategy

I n addition to a good foundation, a home also needs a framework upon which you can build things like a roof and walls.

If your children do not mind you, then you do not have a good framework in place. In this chapter, I will outline a tried-and-true way to bring peace and order back to your home. While the method is very specific, the system provides for complete customization based on your child's age and personality.

Every child is unique. Some children are sensitive and require gentle correction, while others are hard-headed and stubborn and need serious consequences in order to change behavior. I've had the privilege of raising children with both of these dispositions and everything in between.

All great plans are developed over time through trial and error, research and experience.

Each of your children also has different needs, things that motivate them and areas they need to work on improving. These things are ever-changing and require you to pay attention and be flexible with your plan.

Obviously, you can't just send your kids to Grandma's house while you figure out your brilliant comprehensive parenting plan. All great plans are developed over time through trial and error, research and experience.

START RIGHT NOW WITH ONE THING.

For me that one thing was respect. It was our starting place. Your one thing might be different. What's important is that you identify that one thing that you want to change right now.

Write down your one thing that makes you want to pull out your hair on a daily basis.

You will now need a plan for tackling that one thing. And, you are going to stick to this plan like your life depends on it...because it does (well, your parenting plan does anyway).

The elements of your plan will include the following

elements. You decide what those elements should look like:

1. A clear and well-defined age appropriate consequence. Don't make it too complicated. Don't choose something that requires a lot of policing on your part.

2. A single warning. That's one warning and no more. If you give more than one warning, you have failed your plan. (Do not compromise on this point.)

3. Be consistent. That means implement your plan the same way EVERY SINGLE TIME. That means both parents doing it the same way and doing it every single time without fail. That means before coffee, late at night and while you are busy in the middle of something. Regardless of what else is going on, be consistent. Always.

Example:

Your One Thing	Your One Warning Line	Consistent Consequence
Not turning off TV when asked	Would you like to rethink your actions?	Electronic grounding for 24 hours. (No TV or other devices that operate on power or batteries.) Add 24 hours for every instance of disrespect, talking back, or arguing that occurs following first consequence.

Write down your one thing:

Your One Thing	Your One Warning Line	Consistent Consequence

This is what this will look like in action:

SCENARIO #1

Mom: "Johnny, please shut off the TV and come sit down for dinner."

Johnny: "But mom, my favorite show is on."

Mom: "Would you like to rethink your actions?"

Johnny: "But I want to finish my show." [whining]

Mom: "You have now chosen a 24-hour electronic grounding. Now, please shut it off and come for dinner."

Johnny: "That's not fair. I just wanted to finish my show." [more whining]

Mom: "I'm sorry that you've chosen to argue with me. (<= underscores child's control over situation) You have now added a second 24 hours of electronic grounding. (<= underscores parent's control over situation) Would you like to rethink your actions now?"

Johnny: "Yes, ma'am."

SCENARIO #2

Mom: "Johnny, please shut off the TV and come for dinner."

Johnny: "Do I have time to finish my show?"

Mom: "No, I'm sorry we are waiting for you to eat."

Johnny: "But it's almost over."

Mom: "Would you like to rethink your actions."

Johnny: "Yes, ma'am."

When Johnny asks Mom if he could finish his show, she then decides if that would be appropriate. This way Johnny is learning to communicate his wishes respectfully or to respond appropriately when he doesn't get his own way.

To implement your plan you need to do the following:

- Get your spouse to buy into the plan and agree to implement it with you.
- Have a family meeting and let the kids know that this is how things are going to work with your one thing from now on.
- Post the one thing, warning line and consequences on the fridge so everyone is clear.

HOMEWORK: Go implement a plan on your one thing. Make a commitment to yourself and your kids to put it into action. Give one warning. Be consistent. Use your warning line—do not threaten. DO NOT FAIL on this one thing. We are not working on anything else but this one thing.

(Elevator music here)

Ok, so how did it go?

AWESOME! I knew you could do it! Are you excited about the results? Are you ready to take it to the next level? Yes! Let's take it the next level!

When my submissive only child was 11 years old, we adopted a sibling group of four children from the foster care system. It goes without saying that these sweet souls came from a very different background and experience than my daughter.

I learned quickly that we had many things to work on teaching my new additions. Even the basics like table manners, following directions or even just a few house rules were a foreign concept. The impact of going from an only child to five children overnight was overwhelming. However, I knew that I couldn't fix everything at once so I had to work to narrow it to something manageable.

I hate to admit it, but from the outset my kids were pretty rude and often mean. To each other. To me. To anyone who crossed their path. To be honest, I thought I was going to lose my mind. They argued with me about everything. They ignored me when I asked them to do something. They fought with each other about anything and everything. They hit each other. They cursed at each other. They made me want to stay on the floor of my closet and not come out ever again. (Anyone been here?)

I needed something to help me address the day-to-day issues of willful disobedience, disrespect and talking back. The idea of making a chart of each behavior, warning and consequence for every situation was too cumbersome. I needed a simple way of implementing a framework of discipline that could be used in the heat of the moment.

THE TICKETS

The Tickets saved my life. I am certain I would have gone mad. I have shared this concept with many friends and family over the years and it's always proven very successful when implemented correctly and consistently. Better still, it's simple. I like simple. I need simple.

Starting at about five years of age through high school, the Ticket system can be the basic framework for your parenting plan. Children younger than five years are not a good fit yet with the Ticket System because they need more immediate consequences.

While you may choose other reward/consequence systems for specific situations, the ticket system gives you a starting point upon which to build. In other words, start here and get this system working effectively and you will have greater success with anything else you implement down the road.

The Ticket System uses the elements of your "one thing plan"—behavior, warning, consequences. Now that you have practiced giving one warning and giving consequences with your one thing, you are ready to take it to the next level and implement it across the board.

Tickets are simply slips of paper. I used a Word document in which I typed all the list of consequences. These consequences were built around the concepts of personal responsibility, serving your family and stewardship. Tickets were kept in a container in a central location of the house.

Ticket contents included:

- Copying out Scripture verses that speak to the concepts I wanted them to learn. Younger children can write out the verse one time by copying it from a sheet of paper. Older children write it out 20 times and provide a verbal explanation of what it means to them.

- Essays on responsibility, serving and stewardship. For younger children it might be drawing a picture of something that shows that concept, then when they can, assemble sentences into a 50-word essay. Older children can write 200 words or more on the subjects.

- Chores built around the idea of serving the family. Making a sibling's bed, vacuuming the playroom floor or doing someone else's chores for them.

- Chores that made my life easier. I loved coming up with strange chores like dusting baseboards, wiping down switch plates or organizing the pots and pans cabinet. This was stuff I didn't have time to think about and this way it got done eventually.

- Mercy tickets. About 10 percent of my tickets were mercy tickets. This was a free pass on consequences. This teaches them what mercy feels like on the receiving end. They know they deserve a consequence and it makes an impression on them to be given grace. My kids actually came up with the mercy dance for when they pulled a mercy "ticket." Sometimes we would high-five and I'd let them know that God was blessing them today. And sometimes I was really annoyed they got the mercy ticket because I was looking forward to them receiving a consequence. It was a lesson in trusting God and self-control for me!

I had two phrases that worked as my established warnings for all things. I needed a pre-planned response otherwise they were confused about whether or not they were being warned. This way they knew when they heard either "Would you like to rephrase?" which was for verbal issues or "Would you like to rethink that?" which was for behavior issues.

I asked my stepdaughter not long ago if she'd like a ticket after she said something inappropriate. She replied by stating "You are supposed to say 'Would you like to rephrase?'"

She was right. I apologized and asked her if she'd like to rephrase. She did. We moved on. Kids are more secure when they know the rules. If you are consistent, it will make a world of difference to them.

WHY GIVE A WARNING?

I've read the books on first response obedience. While it may have its merits, it can start to feel like a military base instead of a home and you find yourself making a judgment about whether they were willful in their disobedience or just forgetful and making exceptions. Kids need reminders. Their brains are not fully developed and let's face it, they are very distracted by everything. Warnings serve to give them an opportunity to make a choice. When they choose poorly, they bring the consequences on themselves. I'm fond of saying "I'm sorry that you are choosing to receive a consequence" to reinforce the idea that they are in control. They can obey or they can pay the consequence. It puts the responsibility back with the child and relieves you of the burden.

On the other end of the spectrum, if you give more than one warning you have lost all credibility. Children will push until they meet resistance. They need to know where the line is and that it will not be moved for any reason. This is where they will feel safe and secure.

That doesn't mean they won't test the boundary from time to time. I had one child continue to talk back until she had 12 tickets. I think she just wanted to know if I'd give up at some point. To her displeasure she discovered that I was way more determined to keep my consistency than she was to break me. She didn't test that theory again. Be prepared to go the distance if your child decides to find out how many tickets they can get in one situation.

THE 10 MINUTE TIME-OUT

Sometimes a cooling-off period is needed before additional tickets are discussed. If after giving them one ticket, you clearly see that they are not in control of their emotions, offer them a 10 minute time-out to get themselves together before continuing. It's their option. Simply ask them, "I can see that you are very upset. Would you like a time-out to get yourself together before we continue discussing what happened?" Again, it becomes their choice. If they decline the time-out, then continue with tickets. If they get a few more tickets, you can choose to give them the option for a time-out again. If they choose the time out, they can go to a quiet place (like their room or a designated quiet area) for 10 minutes. Depending on the child, you may want to set a timer so they know when to come back out.

It is also acceptable for YOU to give yourself a time-out to calm down. If you feel so upset about what has happened that you are not able to give consequences without anger, then declare a time out for yourself. Simply say, "I am very upset about what happened and I need 10 minutes to calm down before we discuss it. Please come back in 10 minutes."

Most of the time kids are smart enough to know that if you are that upset, they do not want you making decisions about their consequences in that moment.

Know that in the beginning it will take more work to be consistent.

IMPLEMENTING THE TICKETS

Putting the Tickets into effect in your house will CHANGE EVERYTHING. Before I started doing this my house was chaos. I was exhausted and tired of being sucked into arguments I could never win. I felt like a nag, a broken record and a drill sergeant all rolled up into one scary mommy bundle of frayed nerves.

Know that in the beginning it will take more work to be consistent. Your kids will need time to adjust to the new boundaries you are setting. If you make this investment, you will reap the reward of a more peaceful house, happier kids and a little more sanity in your day. IT IS WORTH YOUR EFFORT.

Too often parents get overwhelmed, too tired or just plain distracted and the system falls apart. You need to treat this system with the priority your family deserves. Stick with it for a week or two and you will discover amazing changes happening within your family.

HOW TO MAKE IT WORK

Remember the elements of your plan: behavior, one warning, then consequences.

Here are a few tips to ensure you are successful:

1. ONE WARNING. And only one. Did I mention only one warning?

2. CONSISTENT WARNING PHRASES. Decide what you are going to say each and every time. Make it the same so your kids will instantly know they are being warned. Don't use questions like "Would you like a ticket?" or "You are about to get into trouble." Do use phrases that reinforce a decision like "Would you like to try rephrasing or rethinking that?" and use the same one consistently.

3. USE TIME-OUTS when needed. Nothing is productive if you or your child are not in control of your emotions. Come back to the discussion when everyone is calm.

4. THROW THEM OUT each time a ticket is pulled and completed. This way you won't have tickets repeated. When the last ticket is pulled, simply print off your

list again.

5. POST YOUR RULES. Make sure everyone is on the same page and understands what is expected of them.

6. DON'T GET SUCKED INTO ARGUING and forget to give them a ticket each time. You are the adult so you must remain calm and in control. One warning, then ticket, then ticket, then ticket, then ticket. There are no more warnings.

7. BE LOVING while you give consequences. No anger. No raised voice. Just sadness that they are choosing to receive consequences. If you can't do it without anger, see number three above. To be honest, this system was so empowering to me that I often found myself smiling through the process. For some reason the kids found the fact that they couldn't get me mad frustrating on their part—which made me smile even more. I'm evil like that.

8. BALANCE WITH PRAISE. Don't forget to give out praise. Praise for getting self-control quickly and only getting one ticket. Praise for not getting a ticket at all. Praise. Praise. Praise.

9. DO NOT THREATEN with a ticket when they are doing something they shouldn't. Use your warning line each and every time. You will be tempted so say things like "Stop that or you will get a ticket." I've done it and I know it will undermine what you are trying to do.

Give them the established warning line instead so the decision for the right choice is being provided instead of a threat of punishment. There is a difference being a warning and a threat.

Some children are easily corrected with a firm "no" while others require Armageddon to even look up from what they are doing.

THE YOUNGER YEARS

From birth through five years of age, children are growing and developing at such a rapid rate. They are taking in everything around them and testing any and all boundaries. They are high energy, emotional and full of spirit.

My personal experience with toddlers is that they are eager to please, lovable and full of curiosity. The greatest consequence they can face is disappointing their parents, followed closely by not getting their own way.

Again, each child is so different. Some children are easily corrected with a firm "no" while others require Armageddon to even look up from what they are doing. You must make your decisions based on the needs of each of your children.

Until they are talking well enough to have basic dialogue, you should communicate consequences firmly, but also give them plenty of praise when they do what you ask of them.

Younger children have short attention spans and are typically very hard of hearing (or suffer from selective hearing syndrome). However, this is a crucial time for establishing firm boundaries and creating habits that will serve you both well as your child grows older.

Most children are eager to please and this age group is no exception. Here's an idea for a simple system which incorporates both a reward for good behavior and a consequence for bad behavior.

BUILD A FACE

Announce that you are going to make a craft with your child. Hurray, crafts! This will be fun and you will get to spend some time together. Tell your child that you will be making a face and see if they would like to do their own face, an animal or something else of their choice. Then gather your materials such as paper plates, yarn for hair, buttons for nose, eyes, stickers and markers/crayons.

On one paper plate you will create a happy face. On a second paper plate, the face will be sad. Glue or tape a string on the inside so it forms a loop for hanging, then tape or staple the two plates together so they face outward.

Hang the plate in a visible place in your home (fridge door, child's door, etc.). When the child is having a good behavior day, have the happy face showing. If they are showing poor behavior, turn the plate over to show the sad face. Tell the child that when they show you good behavior, they can have the happy face showing again.

If your child moves beyond caring whether the face is happy or sad, you can provide incentives for staying on "happy" for a specified period. For example, if your child stays on "happy" until lunch time, they get to have some special time with you or whatever rewards you generally use. Then if they stay on "happy" until bedtime, they can have 20 minutes extra time before they have to go to bed (or again some other small reward of your choosing). This way if they get a "sad" in the morning, they can still earn something in the afternoon.

You can take this system a step further by creating a chart that will track the "happy" and "sad" days with stickers or check marks so they can earn rewards over the course of a week. For example, 10 or more "happy" faces in a week earns an ice cream run with mom or dad to celebrate or to pick a small toy from the dollar store from a "treasure" bin you stock.

TIME-OUT PLACE

Toddlers can get pretty emotional and sometimes just need an opportunity to cool down in safe way. A time-out place can provide a safe location for this to happen. I used a mat because it was portable anywhere in the house or outside on the patio.

Give praise for improvement.
Give praise for effort.
Give lots of praise.

You can also easily take it camping or to Grandma's house.

Depending on their age you can either try reasoning with them first, give them an ultimatum (change behavior now or sit on the mat) or take them immediately to the mat. If you give them an ultimatum, count to three before acting to give them a warning system. Do not restart your counting or give empty threats. Do not give more than one warning. Keep your credibility intact.

Most experts agree that time-outs should be roughly one minute for every year of age, but again you may want to adjust depending on your child's sensitivity to correction. A timer should be used so everyone knows when the time-out is over. If the child speaks or gets up from the time-out place, start the timer over again. You should do this calmly and without anger, as many times as necessary before your hard-headed toddler realizes that you are way more stubborn than they are.

When they make it through their time-out successfully, give them praise for being a big boy/girl and sitting through their time-out. Then get down eyeball-to-eyeball and have a discussion about why they went to time-out. Ask them to apologize, if one is warranted. Tell them they are forgiven. Give lots of hugs and move on with your day.

Give praise for improvement. Give praise for effort. Give lots of praise. Toddlers shine in the glow of doing something right. Give them a reason to make the right choices. Praise. Praise. Praise. Some days it will be harder to dig for something to praise them over but try and find it wherever you can. Think of your praise as the balance to the "no's" and time-outs. Praise needs to be on the winning side and for some children that's going to mean a lot of praise, if you know what I mean. If you feel like all you do is scold your child, then that's probably how it feels to them too.

When my husband and I were dating, his daughter was just four years old. She was quite feisty and prone to wild temper tantrums. The first time I took her shopping resulted in one of the wild temper tantrums happening in aisle four of the toy department. She demanded that I buy her a toy and I said no. She screamed through the toy department, the clothing department and all the way through the food aisles while I did some grocery shopping. She screamed through the check-out line and out to the car. She passed out from what could only be exhaustion before I drove out of the parking lot.

On my second trip to that same store, I was prepared. Before we exited the car, I outlined the ground rules for her.

I was not going to buy her a toy and she was not going to pitch a fit. I'd like to say those words of wisdom were all it took but hey, she was four years old. She spotted something she wanted and made her demands. I said no. She started to pitch a fit but it was a lower-grade fit with crying and no screaming. Since it was an improvement, I decided to focus on that. I picked her up and carried her through the store, whispering in her ear every now and then how proud I was of her for doing so much better than last time.

On our third trip, we started out with the same discussion. No toy. Clear? Clear. We had no issues on that shopping trip and I stopped for ice cream on the way home to celebrate her win. Sometimes all we have is a little progress to celebrate and that's ok. Our kids need us to cheer them on even when the progress is slow.

STICKER CHARTS

I love sticker charts and so did my kids, especially when they were younger. There is just something about stickers that really appeal to kids. Even a toddler can be encouraged to brush their teeth, make their bed or pick up their toys if there is a sticker "reward" in it for them.

Reward charts are super easy to make. Just buy a small piece of poster board. Personalize it with your child's name: Johnny's Chore Chart. Put three activities down the left that you would like to reward them for achieving on a daily basis. Draw a box around the outside leaving a margin for decorating. Let little Johnny decorate his chore chart. Hang in his room, on the fridge or in another prominent location. Each night give little Johnny about a 30-minute heads up that it's almost "chore chart time." This is his clue to go get those things accomplished if he wants to get a sticker for it.

At chore chart time, make a big deal of every sticker. If they don't do anything to get a sticker, don't give them one. Seriously, don't give them one. Don't help them do the activity either. Yes, I'm speaking to you helicopter moms—you know who you are. The reward is for doing it on their own, not because you made them. You can still make them if it's something they need to do, just don't give them a sticker for it.

Again, like with the happy/sad face activity, if more incentive is needed then you can create rewards for a certain number of stickers earned on a weekly or monthly basis. If you offer incentives, be sure to follow through. If you say something, do it. Don't be too busy or distracted to keep your word to your children. You will lose credibility if you do. Your credibility is what makes your word to them mean something. Don't be a flake.

Based on my experience, here are a few things you may want to consider before deciding on a reward/consequence system for your kids.

1. Personalize It. Your kids are unique individuals. Therefore, what works for someone else may need some tweaking before it will be effective with your kids. Also, age and maturity play a factor in how you should approach your system.

2. **Balance It.** If you are only about consequences, your kids will get weary of it all. Motivate them with a system that rewards good behavior as well. Oh, and make sure you follow through on those rewards or you will lose credibility and your system will be worthless.

3. **Be Consistent.** If you don't commit to the system, don't expect your kids to either. If you are very intentional about your consistency, within a few weeks it will be habit for both you and them. It's also important to hold your ground with a single warning. Getting into an argument with a three-year-old is not only impossible to win (and you will look and feel ridiculous), but it also breaks down your entire system. One warning, then apply the consequence. Period. No exceptions.

4. **Keep It Simple.** If it's complicated or requires a lot of policing on your part, it just won't survive the first week. Post the rules and tracking system in a high traffic area so everyone is clear on what is expected and where they stand.

5. **Create Buy-In.** Make sure your spouse is on the same page and understands what you are trying to accomplish. Better yet, make them part of the development process. If they do not understand the system, the kids will quickly learn how to play the other parent to circumvent consequences.

So whether you eat or drink

or whatever you do,

do it all for the glory of God.

1 Corinthians 10:31

Chapter 6

Food Fights

When my kids were younger, I had little tolerance for complaining at the dinner table. With so many going hungry around the world, it upset me that my children were not more grateful for their full bellies. I soon instituted a few of those handy "guidelines" for the dinner table that helped them adjust their attitudes. Of course, the following were my guidelines and I'm only sharing them with you to give you some ideas. You should make your own guidelines for your family.

- **Check It At The Door:** The only acceptable term allowed was "not keen on it." Words such as nasty, yucky or ewww were not permitted. Phrases such as "I ain't eating that!" or "What kind of crap is this?" were also on the not permitted list. Tongues sticking out and nose wrinkles were considered sign language for the afore-mentioned phrases. Those who could not contain their comments were rewarded with a second helping of whatever had caused their dismay. Additional helpings were added on an as-needed basis and, once on the plate, the food had to be consumed in its entirety. If not eaten at that meal, the leftovers were kindly saved until the next meal...even if that meal was breakfast. I once had one child test my commitment to this rule...she went six meals without eating before she broke down and ate the food she had earned through complaining. She only tested me once on this. Really, you would have to know this child to understand. She tested everything.

- **The Three-Bite Rule:** Everything served had a mandatory three-bite rule.

- **The Exception:** Each child was allowed to pick one food item that was an exception from the three-bite rule or for which they would be provided an alternative if it was the entire meal. For example, I had one child who chose spaghetti sauce as her exception. When we had spaghetti, she would have noodles and cheese. In her 20s now, she still eats her spaghetti this way.

- **No Wasting Food.** If you put it on your plate, you were expected to eat it. They were cautioned to only serve up what they could eat knowing they could get more if

80

they wanted it. The point was not that the food be eaten. I just wanted them to understand its value by not allowing them to waste it. Of course, there was always the option to save it for a snack or the next meal, but nothing else was to be eaten until that food was consumed.

- **Eat a Green:** When we went out to eat, it was often a buffet. It was usually less expensive, the kids could pick what they wanted and eat as much as they wanted. My rule here was they had to "eat a green" which meant at least one fruit or vegetable subject to the Three-Bite Rule. The "two sugar buns" per plate rule was also implemented following a trip to the Chinese buffet where it was apparently thought that eight sugar buns and three green beans constituted a well-balanced meal.

Once these guidelines were implemented, our dinner table was peaceful. Ok, peaceful as in little or no complaining and a new appreciation for the value of food. It was still wonderfully loud and crazy.

Let me just add here that complaining is also rude and insulting to the chef (me). If you don't like it, I don't want to hear about it the entire time I'm eating. So there.

Now that my children are grown, I do find it amusing to see them put a "green" on their plate and eat three bites of something I know they wouldn't choose for themselves. Habits of your childhood are hard to break.

THE PICKY EATER SYNDROME

My stepdaughter falls into the very picky eater category. Because she shares time 50/50 between our house and time with her mom, I needed a strategy where I gained her buy-in and cooperation. A hard-line approach would only create conflict due to the inconsistency caused by her living in two households. A different situation calls for a different strategy. Here are some of the ways I'm using to help her learn to make healthy choices for herself regardless of where she is eating.

- **Eat a Protein.** I was sincerely concerned about this child's health. She seemed to survive solely on carbs and juice. We insist that she eat something with protein at every meal. She is now at the point where she has learned to love a wide variety of whole, unprocessed meats. At first, I had to be willing to substitute the protein being served for an alternative as long as she tried it first. We are stressing that protein will help her grow and be strong and encouraging her to expand her list (see "Chart It" below) and make choices.

- **No complaining.** This poor child has been subjected to my "kids are starving" lecture enough times that she has learned to say "I'm not keen on it" instead of making a face or pitching a fit over its extreme nastiness. If she does complain and I start the lecture, she quickly changes her tune just to avoid having to listen to it. An evil strategy I know, but hey, whatever works.

- **Chart it.** We have implemented a Chow Chart. The chart has category headers for Proteins, Veggies, Fruits and Nuts & Seeds. Each category lists food which she has tried and indicates whether she likes it or doesn't care for it. She is rewarded for each 25 "tries" with a trip to the dollar store for a prize. Since putting the Chow Chart in place, she has tried dozens of food items that she would not have touched before—and surprise, surprise, she has liked more than 80 percent of them. Where she would not even touch a vegetable before, she now enjoys spaghetti squash and baby spinach on a regular basis (her two favorites). After trying butternut squash and okra she declared that she "was not keen on it." The fact she will now TRY IT is a win. The entire family shows interest in her opinion and then we share our thoughts on the food in question (our favorite way to have it prepared, etc.). She feels like she is part of a grown-up conversation and it makes her eager to try something new.

With all humility and gentleness,

with patience, bearing with

one another in love,

eager to maintain the unity of

the Spirit in the bond of peace.

Ephesians 4:2-3

Chapter 7

Bonding Matters

Bonding is that incredible attachment between a parent and their child. As a baby, it is the first model for an intimate relationship that your child will have. It is not something that just happens and is completed, but rather it is a process of building a connection that will continue for a lifetime.

Most of us instinctively perform actions that perpetuate bonding with our children as babies. Things such as:

- Touch
- Movement, such as bouncing back and forth or rocking
- Eye contact
- Vocal expressions
- Meeting a physical or emotional need

It is not something that just happens and is completed but rather it is a process of building a connection that will continue for a lifetime.

Research has shown that the emotional and mental well-being of a child can be greatly impacted by whether they have a strong and healthy bond with one of their parents. With something this important at stake, why not be purposeful about making it a part of your parenting plan?

Here are a few ideas for bonding at different stages of your parenting journey.

BEFORE THEY ARE BORN

1. Keep a journal. Record the details of your pregnancy journey so you can both remember yourself and share with your child when they are older. Include maternity and ultrasound photos.

2. Read them stories and sing to them. It is believed that babies can hear in utero and can recognize the voice of the speaker.

THE FIRST YEAR

1. Skin-on-skin contact is a wonderful way to bond with your baby. It's also shown to reduce crying and support breastfeeding.

2. Do life with your baby. When I was young, our family did a lot of camping. When my brother was just two weeks old, he took his first camping trip. Babies don't have to be a reason to stop doing life.

TODDLERS

1. Get a routine. Toddlers love structure. Having a consistent routine will help them feel secure. Bedtime is an especially good time for a routine. My kids loved the "mummy tuck" routine we did each night. It involved tucked the blankets all around the outline of their body until they looked wrapped up like a mummy. I kept that one up until they were teenagers and even then, sometimes they still let me do it and we'd laugh about it.

2. Explore books. Story time is a great opportunity to bond with your kids. We read some of those books so many times that the covers fell off. Many of those favorites end up creating "private jokes" between you. My kids are now adults but I sometimes use a line from their favorite childhood book in their birthday cards or on a Facebook post.

CHILDHOOD

1. Get a family scent. I learned this bonding secret by accident. I love the smell of apple cinnamon and, when it was an option, I'd choose products with that smell. Between the dish detergent, candles and the little patch you stuck to your furnace filter, our house always smelled like apple cinnamon. On a visit to Cracker Barrel, one of my kids exclaimed, "This place smells like home!" I have since learned that smell is the strongest scent tied to memory. What does your family smell like? (And I'm not talking about after football practice. That's just gross!)

2. Build a long list of traditions. Having a lot of traditions builds a sense of belonging and being a part of something that can be counted on. While most of us do have traditions built around the holidays, you can build every day family traditions as well.

    One of my favorite family traditions was sharing what we loved the most about the persons sitting next to us at the restaurant table while we waited for our food. Other traditions might be how and who blesses the food at each meal, homemade waffles every Saturday morning or a weekly family pizza and game night. (Yes, I realize that every suggestion I just made here revolved around food. My family loves food.)

TEENS/YOUNG ADULT

1. Remind them of their youth. My kids love the little individual reminders of our times together in their childhood. It might be a nickname I would call them or a special book we would read together. Those things continue to bind us together as they have moved into the adult years.

2. Keep the traditions alive. Now that most of our kids are out of the house, we continue to be intentional about keeping up our family traditions. We still have "Family Dinner" once a week and during the summer it's expanded to "Lake Day" each Sunday afternoon.

3. Keep talking. My husband recently introduced something new called "Love Talks." After dinner, we ask thought-provoking questions that each member of the family is encouraged to share their opinion. It might be about their favorite movie and why or their favorite toy from when they were younger. We've gained a lot of insight into our thoughts and perspectives during our Love Talks.

4. Have fun! Recently our family had a group text about the upcoming Lake Day that evolved into a battle of the GIFs. It was hilarious, memorable and was an excellent bonding moment, even though we were apart.

My favorite memory of my grandfather was that he insisted on sitting in the front row of the roller coaster and keeping our arms raised the entire ride. I screamed and laughed. Most important, I never forgot it. Laughter is bonding.

The rain came down,

the streams rose,

and the winds blew and

beat against that house;

yet it did not fall,

because it had its foundation

on the rock.

Matthew 7:25

Chapter 8

Keeping House

In addition to a parenting plan, we also need a plan for running our household. A house out of order is chaotic. And we all know that having kids is enough chaos in itself. By keeping our homes running smoothly, we provide an environment for discipline, teachable moments and hopefully, the possibility of holding onto the last remnants of our sanity.

FEEDING THE MASSES

Life would be so much easier if we didn't have to eat. Just think of all the time we spend choosing recipes, shopping, cooking and cleaning up afterward. For some reason, God thought this idea of daily provision as important for us to practice and so he came up with eating.

When I was a mom to one child, I didn't really need to

By keeping our homes running smoothly, we provide an environment for discipline, teachable moments and, hopefully, the possibility of holding onto the last remnants of our sanity.

know much about cooking. We ate out a lot or when I did "cook" it was more of the "peel-the-film-off-the-plastic-container-and-pop-in-the-oven" kind of cooking.

However, as our family grew and my ideas about healthy eating changed, I found that the soggy chicken Parmesan in the frozen dinner aisle wasn't going to cut it any longer. I decided I needed to raise the bar a bit.

Luckily for me, there are some really smart and capable cooks in the world who have created some awesome ideas for feeding a family on a budget and not take up a bunch of precious time doing it.

Here's a few of my favorite ways to minimize time in the kitchen:

Freezer Cooking: It makes sense that this concept appealed to me. It was so similar to my previous approach except now I was actually making the meals myself instead of buying them pre-made. While it was more work, it was much healthier and less expensive.

Our freezer cooking days were held every six to eight weeks. We often partnered with another large family and worked together to make about 100 meals that we could split. Those days were filled with laughter, instructional moments on doubling (and quadrupling) recipes and memories I would not trade for anything.

Freezer cooking also provided a realistic way for our family to bless others. When someone had a baby, was going through a loss or had surgery, we could arrive with a cooler packed full of meals for a week. When the youth pastor at our church got married, the kids and I filled their freezer and prepared a special recipe book with cooking instructions as our wedding gift to them. When they arrived home from their honeymoon, they didn't have to worry about cooking for several months.

5 Dinners 1 Hour (.com): Now that most of the kids have left home, I don't have as many mouths to feed. However, I do run a business, host a radio show, homeschool my stepdaughter and work with my husband on flipping houses. I'm what most would call busy and so I still need a plan. I recently found 5dinners1hour.com and it has been a great solution to the "what's for dinner?" question. The concept involves a shopping list for five meals and instructions for prepping all the meals in under an hour. Then when you get home after a hard day, just throw a meal in the oven and you're done. Hats off to the lady who started this website.

Slow Cookers: The slow cooker was invented by a Jewish man inspired by his mother's recipe for a traditional Jewish dish that cooks all day. The dish was rooted in the Jewish Sabbath, as it could be put on heat before sundown on Friday night and cook all the way through until the end of Saturday services the next day. The Sabbath was a day of rest and observant Jews were not supposed to do any work, including cooking.

In 2011, Consumer Reports reported that 83 percent of families owned a slow cooker. Add in the fact that they now have removable and disposable liners so you don't even have to clean it, I'd say that's a win all the way around. So dust off that slow cooker and put it to work so you don't have to.

ORGANIZATION

I'm not naturally organized. In fact, I'm more of a day-dreaming procrastinator and so I have to be intentional about staying organized.

Here are some things that have really helped me over the years:

- **Get rid of unnecessary stuff.** When you have kids, they have a lot of stuff including clothes, toys, sporting equipment, etc. They also grow out of all those things about every five days so you get them more stuff. My company recently did some strategic planning with a local library. They had grown and space was at a premium. They instituted a one-in, one-out rule. Once you declutter, consider making a one-in, one-out rule for your family.

- **Write it down.** So much time is wasted looking for information. Write your lists, contacts and other important data and keep it accessible. There's probably an app for that if you like that kind of thing. (No probably about it. OneNote is amazing!)

- **Color code it.** When I worked in the corporate world, I would color code my files so I could quickly put my hands on the information I needed. Yes, you guessed it. I color coded my children. Don't judge until you see the genius of this idea.

Each of my children were assigned a color and whenever possible, I made sure their personal items were in that color. For example, they each were given a set of towels in their color. If I found a wet towel thrown in a corner somewhere, I knew who to call to come and pick it up. This was valuable information for other items too such as lunch boxes, water bottles, Christmas stockings, toothbrushes, backpacks, etc.

- **Find an app for that.** Technology gets a bad rap sometimes. However, you can also use it to your advantage. There are so many wonderful apps that help you manage your time, shopping, planning and just about anything else you can think of. Make technology work for you so you have more time for non-tech things like Legos. Because we all need more time for Legos.

SCHEDULING

Keeping track of your kids is like nailing gelatin to a tree. Just when you think you have a system that works, your family dynamic will shift and you need a new system.

At one point in our parenting journey, I had our days scheduled in 10 minute blocks. It was a dark and overwhelming period in our homeschool journey. Thankfully it was a short season, but their needs for individual attention were so great, it was the best way to keep us focused and on track.

At a minimum, most families need some sort of common calendar even if it's the Horses of the World 12-month wall calendar you got at the dollar store and taped to the fridge. In my world, if it's not on the calendar, it doesn't exist. With a computer in everyone's pocket, it's much easier than it used to be to track and share schedules. Google Calendar has a wonderful phone app that syncs with your computer. The calendar can then be shared with everyone in the family old enough to be responsible for their schedule. This is especially handy when standing in the dentist office and they want to make an appointment. Just pull out the phone and check availability, then enter in your appointment day and time—with reminders. Thank heaven for reminders!

If you are a blended family, a shared Google Calendar can also work well for communicating with your ex-spouse. This is something we do with my stepdaughter's mother and it has been very successful. We both have access to add her activities and schedule to the calendar, as well as pick-up/ drop-off information. It prevents those awkward moments when one family assumes the other is picking her up from theatre rehearsal and you get that call from her teacher wondering if you are on the way…and you're not.

LAUNDRY

Post-adoption the number of loads of laundry I had in a week instantly skyrocketed to between 22 and 26 loads a week. Hampers became buried in large mounds of clothing to never be found again. My dryer was not used to such a heavy demand and began overheating after three consecutive loads in protest. In a desperate attempt to tame the mountain, I bought three 30-gallon trash cans on wheels and labeled them whites, colors and darks. I placed them in the garage and would wheel them to the laundry room as needed. If I could keep the laundry from overflowing over the rim, I could also contain the smell with the garbage can lid.

Socks were a particular challenge. So many feet meant

so many socks! At one point I threw out all the socks and bought bags and bags of the same socks for everyone to make matching easier. Plus if one sock got a hole, we could still use it with another lonely sock. Instead of putting socks away in each child's drawer, I just bought a huge basket and put it in a central spot. We called it The Sock Basket. When you needed a sock, you got it from The Sock Basket. If The Sock Basket ran out of socks, it was time to do more laundry. It was always time to do more laundry.

Folding loads and loads of laundry each week is very time-consuming. I taught my kids how to fold laundry and made it a requirement of TV watching. If you were watching TV, you had to be folding laundry at the same time. Before heading to bed, I'd have them collect whatever folded laundry was theirs and put it away. This was a great help to me and training for them. By age 12, the kids were required to do their own laundry. I know. I'm a monster.

KEEPING HOUSE

And we know that for those

who love God all things

work together for good,

for those who are called

according to his purpose.

Romans 8:28

Chapter 9

Blended Families

Divorce is ugly for everyone in a family. However, it is a reality for the world we live in today and one that I've had to personally walk through with my children.

GETTING THROUGH THE FIRST YEAR

The first year following a divorce is especially tough for both you and your children. It takes time for the shock to wear off, to work through the grieving process and to transition through all the changes that divorce often brings.

If this is where you are right now, then just let me give you a word of encouragement. There is life after divorce. You will make it through it. Your kids will be ok.

No doubt you are worried about your kids, working

through things with your ex-spouse or soon-to-be ex-spouse and overwhelmed by all the changes about to take place. Please hear this one thing. Take care of yourself. Do not be a martyr. Do not go without sleeping or eating. You must stay healthy both emotionally and physically. Your ability to care for your family is depending on you more than ever. You don't have the privilege of letting yourself be swept away by your circumstances.

Do the best you can to make sound decisions and wait on those that don't have to be made until you are stronger emotionally.

It is often advised not to make any decisions after a major loss. The problem with that is there are so many changes that come with divorce and we don't always have the luxury of waiting until we have finished grieving. Do the best you can to make sound decisions and wait on those that don't have to be made until you are stronger emotionally.

Keep your focus on God. My personal motto was Stay Vertical. I told myself this regularly throughout the day to help keep me on track with my perspective. Have an accountability partner that you trust to turn you back to God when emotions threaten to carry you away.

THE EX

When you have children, you have to maintain a relationship with your ex-spouse. You won't want to but it's kind of required when you have kids. It's one of those suck-it-up-and-deal kind of situations.

The stronger your relationship with your ex-spouse, the better your kids will do. Think about that for a second. Then think about what will help you build that relationship now and into the future.

If you think punishing or bad-mouthing your ex-spouse is appropriate, your kids will suffer. If you don't have a handle on your anger or other negative emotions, your kids will suffer. If you become bitter, your kids will suffer.

I know. It's difficult. Adulting is hard. Your kids are worth the effort. Here are some areas that I've found to be helpful in building up ex-spouse relations and creating a more ideal situation for your kids.

1. **Pray.** Every day. Without ceasing. Pray for your ex-spouse, your kids and yourself. Pray that God brings you to a place of peace and forgiveness. Pray for their stepparents. Pray for wisdom, discernment and patience. When in doubt, take it to God in prayer.

2. **Your kids are watching you.** Every action and word that comes from you is being watched and digested by your kids. This is your opportunity to model grace and mercy in a way they will remember well into their adult years.

3. **Kids need both parents.** Unless there is cause for concern, kids need to spend time with both their parents. If you are the custodial parent, you may be tempted to use that power against your ex-spouse. Don't do it. Your kids are not a pawn and their time with the other parent is essential to their emotional and mental well-being. Don't be that parent.

4. **Be nice.** When you say bad things about your children's other parent, they can sometimes internalize it for themselves. Your kids are not the right sounding board for your complaints about your ex-spouse.

5. **Communicate.** Being divorced can be complicated. Whether coordinating schedules or who is buying them what for Christmas, communication will be a key to a successful relationship.

6. **Respect.** You may not respect them as a former spouse but you need to respect them as a parent of your children. Give them the same courtesy that you would want given to you if the custody roles were reversed. Talk to them about what the kids are involved in and invite them to participate where possible.

7. **Give some grace.** Your ex-spouse is not perfect. Guess what? Neither are you. They will sometimes be late, forget or make a parental decision you disagree with. Be flexible. Go with the flow. Forgive and forget. Step off the pedestal. Be gracious.

8. **Be inclusive.** When your child has a play, recital or ball game, let the other parent know. They have just as much a right to be there as you. Don't use this as a way of getting back at them for something. This is about your child having both their parents there to cheer them on, not an opportunity for revenge.

STEPPARENTING

I am blessed to have two wonderful stepchildren. Not only are they 10 years apart in age but they could not be more different. I came into their lives when they were four and 14 years old. At the time of writing this book, they are now 10 and 20 years old. I can honestly say that my relationship with them has changed with time.

Initially, you really want them to like you. During those first initial meetings, we were all on our best behavior, sizing each other up. They would see me as someone their dad might marry one day, and me seeing them as potential step-kids one day. It's an awkward albeit peaceful stage.

You know that blissful moment when you buy a new car? You roll it off the dealer's lot all shiny with that intoxicating new car smell. You drive it around in awe and wonder of its newness. Until the girl at the drive-thru doesn't fasten your coffee lid all the way and it goes flying all over your seats, console and carpet. It's called "the christening" and it is the moment your new car has officially been broken in.

There is also that moment in the stepparenting relationship. That moment when something happens and thereafter your relationship is officially broken in. That's the moment when the honeymoon is over and you really figure out what it means to be a stepparent.

Meet them where they are, not where you want them to be.

WHY IT'S DIFFERENT

Being a stepparent is not like being a parent. You are the outsider. You are starting the relationship with a bonding value of zero. You might even be the first person they have ever seen their parent with other than their biological parent…and that's just weird for them.

The challenges of stepparenting are many and not always immediately apparent. Here are some truths you may not like but you should consider.

1. **You are not in charge.** The parents of your stepkids have the right to decide just about everything concerning their kids. Your authority here is limited only to what is given to you by one or both of them. Those lines can be blurry sometimes, especially if there is not good communication. You can offer an opinion but at the end of the day, the final decision rests with the parents.

2. **Your role is different from being a parent.** Your role is to support your spouse and their decisions. You need to take your cues from your spouse on how they wish to raise their kids. You are not always going to agree but you need to respect their parental right to dictate the boundaries and methods for their children. Trying to insist that your way is the only right way will cause problems in your marriage.

3. **Your relationship will need time to grow.** Biological parents bond with their children before they are ever born. It takes time to develop an intimate relationship. You will need to draw on patience as you navigate different personalities and personal history. Some children are ready and open to building a relationship with a stepparent, while others may still be grieving the loss of their family. Meet them where they are, not where you want them to be.

Whoever receives one such child

in my name receives me.

Matthew 18:5

Chapter 10

The Blessing of Adoption

For 11 years I parented an only child. I spent those first 11 years as a working mom focused on my career. At the time, I said I would never have more children. One was all I thought I could handle. (And this is where God laughed and laughed—and laughed some more.)

When my oldest was 11, I adopted a sibling group of four children ages eight, nine, 10 and 11 years old. For the first six months I spent a lot of time on my knees in my walk-in closet asking God if He might have made a mistake in choosing me for this task. I was beyond overwhelmed with frayed nerves and exhaustion like I had never known. Did I also mention I homeschooled all of them and continued to run a business?

Adoption is a big decision. No one can really prepare you for what to expect. Every child has different needs coming into an adoptive family. Every family adopting has its own unique dynamic.

I've often been asked by those considering adoption if I would do it again. The answer is "Yes, of course!" but it is far from the end of the answer.

I've also been told by observers of our family that I must be a saint and/or possess some superhuman capabilities. The answer to both is "No, not by a long shot!"

Our family was created by God with each member specifically chosen to be put together. While I was on my knees in the closet wondering if I was going to lose my mind, God had a bigger plan. My adoption experience has shown me the creativity in which God works all things together for good.

STARTING WITH ME

Imagine bringing home four kids that you do not know. It was the little things that built up to overwhelm me. Aside from the noise, activity and drama, there were suddenly 24 loads of laundry to tackle each week, along with grocery shopping, cooking and stray single socks! Seriously, I once rounded up all the single socks that had no match. There were 125. It is a mystery to this day how that even happens.

Each of those sweet babies had already been through a lifetime of hurt, abuse and neglect. They were broken and hauling around a huge amount of baggage. This did not change just because some strangers brought them home and declared they now had a "forever family."

It took much longer than I expected to gain a new sense of normal.

Adoption changed me in ways that is hard to describe. It was the hardest thing I have ever faced, with challenges I never could have anticipated. It sharpened my relationship with the Lord as I walked through unfamiliar territory and faced demons I had never before encountered. Those first six months of desperation in my closet taught me to fully rely on God for every thought, every moment and every decision. Without Him, I was lost.

There came a time in my journey when I realized how much I had changed as a result of being blessed with this wonderful family. Each challenge, each obstacle rubbed those sharp edges off my character. I began to understand that God didn't just bring those kids to our family to "save" them, but part of His plan was also to change and grow me. It is humbling to realize that the Creator of the universe cares enough about you to put such a plan in motion.

When people first gave me that "you are a saint" line, I didn't know how to answer. It felt awkward and embarrassed because I knew I was a hot mess and far from a saint. With the benefit of many years behind me and the hindsight that provides, I have a much better response. I can now point to God's design and purpose. Not to create a saint, but rather to mold a broken human into something He could use for His glory.

If you think adoption is just about kids, you might want to rethink your perspective. I can guarantee you that God's plan for your family is much bigger.

THE FIRST FEW YEARS

When you first bring home adopted children, you experience a few weeks of what is called "the honeymoon period." Everyone is in an excited state and on their best behavior. Parents are letting things slide as you are trying to bond and avoid conflict and kids are trying to gain favor and position while trying to figure out what they have been brought into.

However, the newness soon starts to wear off and real life rears its head. As they get comfortable, kids start to test the boundaries and parents realize they must now enforce them. Whatever system you had in place before is no longer valid. The dynamic has changed and you begin the process of trying to figure out how you are going to make it work.

Those first few years were a time of gradually moving toward being settled as a family. We learned. We grew.

We experimented. The one thing I wish I had given both myself and the kids was more grace. It's a process and it takes time. It took much longer than I expected to gain a new sense of normal.

THE BIG CHALLENGES

The small challenges came at me like rapid fire from an AK-47. Having parented an only child, I had to now learn about sibling rivalry, fighting and similar chaos. While it took some adjusting, these small challenges soon became a part of my every life.

However, there were some more difficult challenges that are unique to adoption that are worth discussing.

• Adjusting to the individual preferences was not something I was prepared for. In my case, the number was exponentially greater since there were four individuals new to our family. Before the adoption, I didn't give preferences a second thought because I had grown to know all those intimate details of my family over time.

Whether it be who takes mayo and who hates mustard, or who is a night owl and who is a morning person, these details for me were a little stressful. When I forgot what they took on their sandwiches, I felt like a terrible mother. It did take some time to get all those kind of little preferences straight. It was a lot of information coming at my brain at one time. Might seem silly if you haven't experienced it for yourself but seriously, who doesn't like mayo?

- Laundry for us was a massive change. If you adopt a sibling group, it can be a huge increase in housework, particularly laundry. If you know someone who adopts a sibling group, have a fundraiser and buy them a XXL capacity washer and dryer. Trust me on this. They will call you blessed for years to come.

- Your kids will be grieving. Just by virtue of the fact that they are adopted means they have loss. They will need to grieve and depending on their age, it could present itself in a number of ways. This is so important for adoptive parents to understand and to be aware of so you can identify and address it.

  Each of my kids grieved in a different way. For my kids, it sometimes looked like anger or behavioral issues and other times it was anxiety or sadness. Grieving is a process and it can take years for them to work through all the stages. Your role as a parent is to help keep them moving through the process so they don't get stuck. A counselor or therapist familiar with adoption can help you better understand what your kids are going through and how to help them.

- They may not understand you. As you are learning about this special unique child of yours, they are also trying to figure you out. This can be especially a challenge in an international adoption or even a transracial adoption. There can also be language and communication differences, as well as different cultural or religious conflicts.

My adopted kids are Hispanic. Although they spoke English as a first language, their vocabulary was limited. This is not unusual for kids in their situation. In their early years, they were not invested in or communicated with like those in strong, loving families. They soon told me that they could not understand a lot of what I was saying because I was using words they had not heard before. For the record, I did not change my vocabulary for them. If they didn't understand, I would repeat it for them in a simpler way, but I expected them to learn and grow. As they used "new" words, I started giving them a fist bump. Unexpectedly, it became a way our family encourages each other by giving "props" to those who use a "big" or uncommon word. It was an unspoken game that we play to this day. One time following a fist bump, I had one of my kids say they had been saving that word for the right moment for more than a week! This is a lesson in turning lemons into lemonade. When you are met with a challenge, find a way to make it into a positive experience instead.

1. It's not likely that they will share your values. Regardless of their age at adoption (unless an infant), your adopted

kids will have some ingrained values developed from their previous life. It may not align with yours. In fact, it most likely will not. This means you could hear a few colorful words, be forced to try and make sense of some seriously fuzzy logic or find yourself trying to explain the line between fact and fiction.

2. The best analogy I have heard is one of wild horses. When first brought "home" from the wild, they are afraid and skittish. By spending some time in the large fenced-in pasture, they learn to feel comfortable in their more hemmed-in surroundings. Eventually, they will let you lead them around the corral and at some point, into a stall in the barn.

3. As your kids learn to trust you, they will be more willing to stay inside the boundaries you are setting for them. My youngest daughter was once asked by a social worker if she liked our rules. Even at eight years old she said that the rules made her feel safe. Go ahead and make those boundaries but keep expectations realistic to where they are in their journey.

4. You will need a plan for bonding. Before I brought my adopted kids home, I prayed that God would create a situation where we could effectively bond. Their first week home, three of them came down with a violent stomach bug. Those hours I spent holding barfing children over the toilet is not really what I had in mind, but God

knew what he was doing. After six hours with one of my children on the bathroom floor, they asked me why. I didn't understand the question at first, but when I did I said, "Because that's what moms do." They said they had never had anyone take care of them when they were sick before. I cried and holding that child took on a whole new perspective.

5. They need you to nurture them. As I shared in the previous point, many kids have never had anyone nurture them in a meaningful way. When one of my kids got a "boo-boo," I went overboard on my sympathy and caring for the situation. They needed to know I cared and that even their skinned knees mattered to me. Our skinned knee, splinter and "bonks" routine was so popular with them, they started bringing me random neighborhood children to patch up as well. They said I was "an expert" and would take care of it.

6. The end of the journey may not be what you expect. There are some situations in my adoption journey that are heartbreaking. When you love a little human and allow yourself to be vulnerable, there is a risk of being hurt. You do not have control over everything and sometimes things don't work out the way you desire. Adoption is not all skittles and rainbows.

WHY I'D DO IT ALL AGAIN

As with most things that are difficult, the rewards are great. My kids are one of my greatest blessings and I'm thankful for every day I have been given to be their mom. I have been given the gift of seeing them conquer their demons and find freedom in the saving knowledge of Jesus Christ. They were each created for a plan and a purpose and watching God work in their lives would be reason enough to do it all again.